Against All Odds

A story of survival

By Martha Philbeck

HOME OF THE GOLDENPAWS
www.homeofthegoldenpaws.com

Against All Odds

This will be a story of survival. The parents picked out my pond to raise their young. They swam around for several days looking for the right spot.

They made a nice nest on a ledge on the side of the steep bank. The ledge was not very wide and dropped down sharply to the water. The mother pulls out her feathers to make a soft bed for the eggs and to cover them when she gets off of the nest.

A bad storm came with 4 1/2 inches of rain.   It washed one of the eggs into the pond, you can see the washed out path it took. It also took all the feathers out of the nest that she had to protect and cover the eggs.

The eggs were just lying on the bare dirt. The parents worked very hard trying to get the egg back into the nest. The other eggs got very cold while they tried. Finally the mother got back onto the nest. Then a week later an animal got into the nest and took two eggs onto the bank at 1:30 in the morning. Around nine I brought the rest of the eggs in and put them in an incubator. The parents were too afraid to go back to the nest. It had been abandoned. The eggs were very cold and I did not know if they would still survive.

On April 8th, I could hear the chatter of one of them talking and trying to get out. The other egg also started to talk back and forth and they worked on pecking a hole to escape their prison of the shell.

The egg on the left is just starting to get a crack in the shell. The one on the right you can see the raised area. The eggs are very dirty since they had been lying on the ground. You do not want to wash or try to clean up the eggs. The shell is porous and if you tried to clean up the eggs it would get into the pores of the shell and the baby could not breathe.

You can see how they have pecked a circle all around the shell and lifted the lid to come out.

This morning about 5:30 I awoke to the happy sounds of them as they reached their freedom. They were having a celebration of life. I was greeted with the sounds of the two survivors when I opened up the top of the incubator. They were not completely dried off. They are truly a miracle with all that happened to them before they got here. I had put 4 eggs in the incubator and 2 of them did not survive. So the story of Romeo and Juliet the second begins. It is April 9th, 2013.

Hello World

At the sound of my voice they both scrambled closer to see me. They were very tired and weak. It takes them about 24 hours to gain their strength and dry off. They will soon be moving to a bigger home where they can move around more and stand up tall.

They sleep a lot to get their strength. As they get stronger they move around more.

Out for their first stroll. They have been playing in their water
bowl. They grow very fast. They take their first swim in the sink.

They love splashing in the water. They are a week older. You can already see the change in color. I am feeding them a granular feed for turkeys and ducks and starting to mix in some cracked corn.

At 2 weeks of age it is warm enough to start taking them outside during the day. They love eating the grass. Each day I moved the cage so they had clean grass to eat.

Notice the change in color by the time they are 4 weeks old. They are mostly grey. Their legs are getting longer and see how big their feet are. I used an old hydrator pan for them to drink out of. They get in it and try to take a bath.

15

They are so happy when I let them out in the morning that they have to stretch their wings and try to fly.

At 5 weeks they are starting to get their pin feathers or first feathers.

See how they are starting to get their feathers. They loose their baby fuzz. They really look shaggy at this stage. Romeo loves to talk to me. See how big his tongue is as he greets me.

They love to watch me and see what I am doing.

You can see in this picture that they still have some baby fuzz to loose around the neck and head. Romeo is always the first to do anything. He meets me first and talks the loudest to me.

By six weeks they have almost totally changed their color and have their white cheeks. Romeo is a little bigger than Juliet.

The white feathers above the tail are down like the mother pulls
out to line the nest. They look very soft and fluffy.

All Grown Up

Setting in the weeds she is hard to see. They are now full grown by the first of July and their voices are starting to change.

She likes to try and hide.

Each morning they are overjoyed to see me and stretch their wings to show me how big they are getting. Compare this picture to the earlier one of the wingspan.

First attempt at flying. They cannot go very far at first.

Each day they Get better and stronger. They have a 5 foot wing span.

The Visitors

Behold July 21, 2013 the parents return.

The father talks to Romeo and convinces him to follow.

His father is in the corner of the pen and shows Romeo how to jump the fence. The three of them left and Juliet has waited and called but Romeo does not return. Other visitors come in but she ignores them.

Juliet's Wait

She looks and calls and he does not come. She tries to fly and hits the side of the house and falls down on the deck. She has to be rescued.

She knows she has to practice. She cannot go very high.

The more she practices the better she gets.

She can now fly over the house.

The search for Romeo

She thinks she has found him. They have hidden him in the house. She sees him when she looks in the window.

She takes a closer look.

She looks in the yard.

Juliet's first swim was August 10, 2013. Other geese come in and try to get her to swim. She does not seem to like the water.

She does like Casper and sometimes sleeps with him. She pecks the hair on his chest.

Winter comes

The first snow has fallen. Juliet does not like to walk in it. It is cold.

Her feet get cold so she stands on one foot and holds the other one up. Sometimes she tucks her nose under her wing.

The weather is getting colder and there are only small patches of water left. She starts to walk to the bank and falls through the ice.

35

She slowly eases her body back onto the ice and walks a little farther.

She stretches her wings in joy as she nears the bank.

Her feet get cold again and she sets on them to warm them up. She will be glad when spring and warm weather returns. She now knows why the geese tried to talk her into migrating with them.

The Chase

Juliet has had the pond to herself. One day another pair flies in and decides it is their pond. They do not want her on the pond. They have decided this is the perfect place to raise a family.

She tries to get away but he insists that she get out of the water.

He chases her all the way to the bank. She hurries to escape.

As she leaves the water they are scolding her.

The pair rejoices that they have managed to get her out of the water and claim their pond.

Juliet preens her feathers after the fight

She goes up to the house where she feels safe and starts to groom her feathers. First she must shake the water off.

Then she stretches her wings.

Then she strokes her tail feathers.

Finally she is as pretty as she can be. It may be awhile before she is brave
enough to go to the pond again.

Juliet and the Nut Hunter

Juliet hears a noise and sees someone walking down the drive. Out of curiosity she follows. She needs to know what is going on all the time. She has a family to protect. There he is standing under the tree looking for something.

She decides to look too.

What did you say you were looking for?   Nuts?

She sees some lying on the grass.

She thinks that she sees another one.

She buries her head under the leaves to try and pick it up but her mouth is not big enough. Dad seems to have more luck than she does at picking up nuts. She can roll them out for him to see.

He has both hands full of nuts as he tries to get the hull off of them. She is working hard hunting nuts when she hears a noise. The 4 wheeler has started up. Oh, no she must hurry to catch up with it. Mom is leaving.

She goes as fast as she can. She has almost caught up with the bike. She knows she must go faster to keep up.

She really must hurry to keep up.

As they go out of site she is right behind the 4 wheeler her favorite place to be. She learned how to fly by going fast along side of it.

Juliet and the fisherman

She patiently stands and waits for him to catch a fish. She loves his company. She knows to stay out of his way when he is casting for fish. The line has hooks on it.

She eats dandelion greens as she waits for him. Oops he is leaving and she almost missed it. You can see her wings as she hurries to follow him around the pond. After all she is his fishing buddy.

Other books by Martha.

This is the story in easy steps of the life and family and birth and nurturing of the Canadian goose. In easy to understand language you learn about the habits and needs of the Canadian goose and how to raise the young. Full knowledge about the eggs and their incubation is also included.

THE CANADIAN GOOSE
BY MARTHA PHILBECK

goldenpaws@embarqmail.com
www.homeofthegoldenpaws.com

Hey Grandma
there's a Bird in this Egg

By Martha Philbeck

53

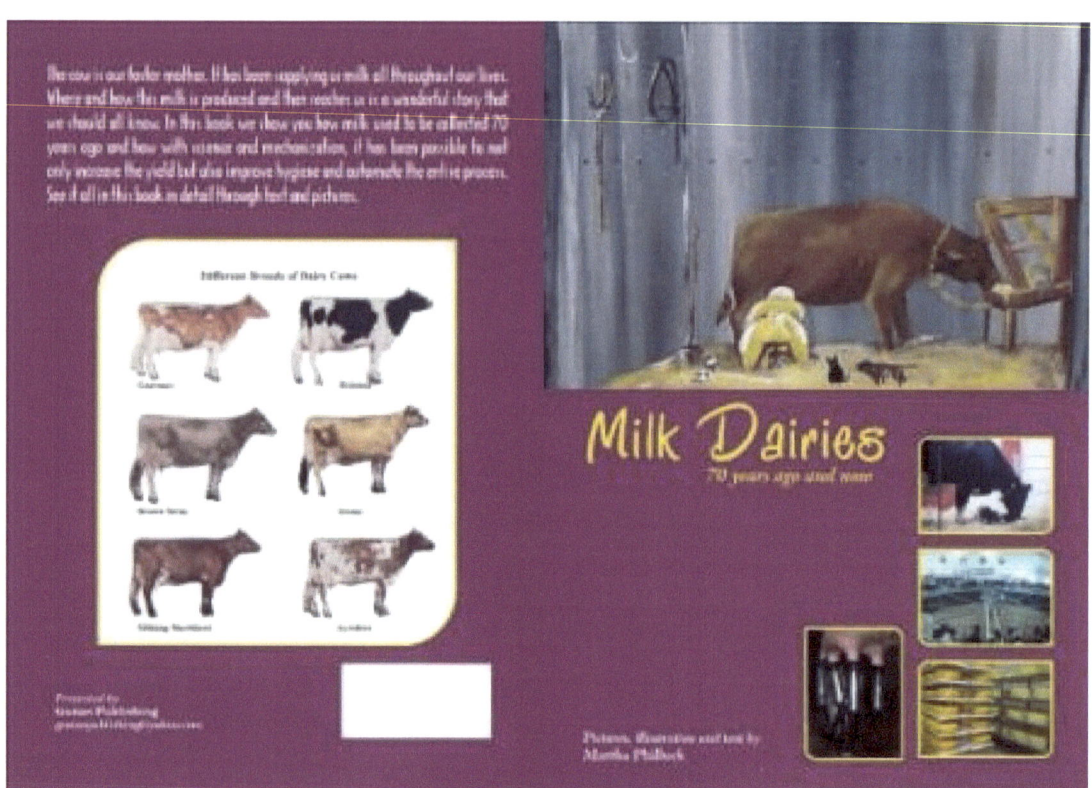

Milk Dairies
70 years ago and now

Pictures, illustration and text by
Martha Philbeck

WILDLIFE ON MARTHA's FARM

The farm is a place of solace where we can connect with
nature and vibrant life.

Pictures and texts by Martha Philbeck.

THE GOLDEN BOOK OF
GOLDEN RETRIEVERS

A compendium of their History, Raising and Training

By Martha Philbeck

A lovely story of a goose that found it difficult to take off but did not give up. By sheer dint of will power and application he did finally manage to fly of course, with the help of his father!

The Goose that could not Fly

Promoted by:
Goose Publishing
goosepublishing@yahoo.com

USA

By Martha Philbeck

Poignant stories by children and for children; an interesting and heart rending collection.

Charlie Coyote and other stories
Volume 2

By Martha Philbeck

Promoted by Gunas Publishing
gunaspublishing@yahoo.com

Monarch Butterflies

Messengers of the Great Spirit

By Martha Philbeck

Martha's *Farmhouse Cuisine....*
Recipes from the 1900s for the kitchens of 2000s

Collection of Main Dishes,
Farmhouse Wisdom and much more

By Martha Philbeck

Martha's *Farmhouse Cuisine....*
Martha's Special collection of

Countryside Desserts...
Recipes from the 1900s for the kitchens of 2000s

By Martha Philbeck

57

Charlie Coyote and
other short stories.

Martha Philbeck & others

Love is a Puppy,   By Jim Philbeck

Love is a puppy given by God
Love is a puppy, Dixie is her name.
Love is a puppy that comes with a nod
Love is a puppy; she's the one I claim

Love is a puppy, I'll lose her someday
Love is a puppy, I adore her so.
Love is a puppy, God keep her I pray,
Love is a puppy, I know she must go.

Love is a puppy; I had never had before,
Love is a puppy, I'll never have again.
Love is a puppy; she is ever so pure,
Love is a puppy, thank you Father. Amen

Martha and Jim are farmers, with a creative personality. Martha is a Great cook , creative artist
and lover of Nature. She is into art, handicrafts and many other things.

THE ADVENTURES OF
LOVIE AND FRIENDS
Remembering a great friend

Martha Philbeck

Barcode Area
We will add the barcode for you.
Made with Cover Creator

www.ingramcontent.com/pod-product-compliance
Lightning Source LLC
Chambersburg PA
CBHW040307010626
45792CB00025B/1159